4/97

Muscular
Dystrophy

Expert Review by
Stephen D. Rioux, M.D.

GAIL

LEMLEY

BURNETT

Crestwood House
Parsippany, New Jersey

HEALTH ■ WATCH

Acknowledgments

With thanks to:

■■■■ Stephen D. Rioux, M.D., Director of the Muscular Dystrophy Clinics in Maine and Pediatric Neurologist, for his advice and review of this book.

■■■■ Scott and Louis Parker, Michael Norton, and their families for their willingness to share their stories.

Photo Credits

Cover: *l.* Carl D. Walsh. *m.* Karen Fucito/The Daily Record. *r.* John W. Karapelou/Phototake. Graphic courtesy of Muscular Distrophy Association: 20. The Daily Record/Karen Fucito: 30. Courtesy, Muscular Dystrophy Associaiton: 11, 28, 36, 39, 40, 42, 43. Carl D. Walsh: 7, 8, 9, 16, 25, 26.

Cover and book design by Lisa Ann Arcuri

 Published by Crestwood House, A Division of Simon & Schuster, 299 Jefferson Road, Parsippany, NJ 07054

First Edition
Printed in the United States of America
10 9 8 7 6 5 4 3 2 1

Library of Congress Cataloging-in-Publication Data
Burnett, Gail Lemley.
   Muscular Dystrophy / by Gail Lemley Burnett.
      p.   cm. — (HealthWatch)
   Includes bibliographical references and index.
   ISBN 0-89686-864-8
      1. Muscular dystrophy—Juvenile literature. [1. Muscular dystrophy. 2. Diseases.]   I. Title.   II. Series.
RC935.M7B87   1996
616.7'48—dc20
94–27370

Summary: Discuss the causes, effects, and treatment of muscular dystrophy, a genetic disease that causes slow weakening of the muscles.

Contents

Chapter 1

The Family Disease

Scott Parker looked like a normal, healthy baby when he was born 20 years ago. But something wasn't right.

His mother, Louise, could tell by the way he acted. Scott's older brother, who was adopted, had been alert as an infant. But Scott, she says, seemed limp and "just slept for six months after he was born."

Because he didn't move around much, he gained more weight than an average baby. But his doctors weren't too concerned. When Scott started to walk, his mother and father, James, became more worried. Scott tried to walk on tiptoe. Instead of falling down on his bottom like other babies, Scott stiffened and fell straight back. He often bumped his head on the floor.

That was when the doctors decided to test Scott. The tests showed Scott had **muscular dystrophy (MD)**. His muscles would keep getting weaker for the rest of his life.

Scott's parents had suspected their son had muscular dystrophy even before the diagnosis. While she was pregnant, Louise Parker had had problems. Her muscles ached. When she walked or was active for a while, her legs felt stiff. Her two sisters and brother had had the same problem years earlier.

"The minute I'd sit down, I'd have the stiffness back again," she recalls.

Doctors at first said her legs hurt because of her pregnancy, but Louise felt it was something else. And the condition continued after Louise gave birth. From her own symptoms and Scott's, she knew that she and her son were going to be like her sisters and brother. Doctors had already told them that they had a form of muscular dystrophy. It seemed to be a family trait.

Compared with many families with muscular dystrophy, Louise Parker's family is lucky. The form of the disease they share takes a long time to worsen. It usually starts between ages 20 and 40. (Scott's illness began when he was a baby.) People who

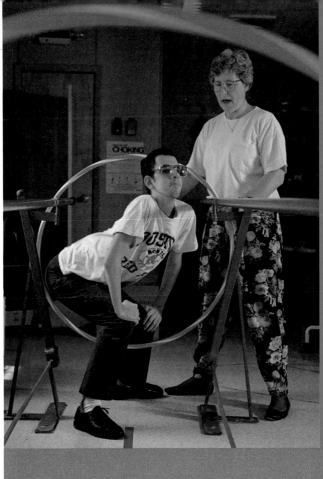

Scott Parker, who has muscular dystrophy, is aided by his physical therapist Barbara Gould in an exercise to improve his body mechanics.

have it can live to be at least 60 or 70.

Almost 20 years later, Louise and Scott Parker are both still walking, with help. Louise now needs someone to help her rise to a standing position and has to have rails or someone's arm to hold onto when she walks. She is able to go grocery shopping with her husband. She holds onto the cart for support.

Her disease gets worse slowly. Her condition remains the same for months at a time. Then, "all of a sudden, you notice something else you can't do." She doesn't want to use a wheelchair until she has to.

Scott will probably have a harder time because he had MD at birth. He has mild mental retardation. At age 20, he reads about as well as a fourth-grader.

So far, Scott can walk with **leg braces**. He can also ride a bicycle and a horse. He doesn't like to talk about his disease. For several years, he has gone to a special

Scott Parker removes the braces that help support his lower legs.

school for physically handicapped children in Portland, Maine, near the family's home in Waterboro. He has held some part-time jobs.

Louise Parker says she and her son aren't ready to lie down and be sick. She moves around every day. So does Scott. When she can, she works in the garden. The way MD affects a person "depends on whether you give up or not," Louise Parker says. The Parkers are not giving up.

Chapter 2

What Is Muscular Dystrophy?

Every time people move, and even when they don't, they use muscles. There are more than 500 large and small muscles throughout the body. They control everything from breathing to kicking a football.

There are two basic kinds of muscles: voluntary and involuntary. **Voluntary muscles** are the ones you move on purpose. The muscles in your legs, used every time you walk or run, are voluntary muscles. These muscles are also called skeletal muscles. They are connected to the bones that they help to move.

Involuntary muscles work whether you think about them or not. They include the heart, which beats on its own, and the muscles in your intestinal system, which help to digest your food. You don't have to tell the muscles to do their job. They just do it.

In muscular dystrophy, the voluntary muscles become weak and break down. This happens over a period of years—sometimes many years, sometimes only a few. The muscles become weaker and flatter, so the person can do less and less with them.

As the disease worsens, the person has trouble moving the muscles affected by MD. Some kinds of muscular dystrophy affect the leg muscles. Other kinds affect the arm muscles. Still others affect the muscles of the face. In some cases, the disease eventually spreads to almost all the muscles in the body.

After a person has had MD for many years, the muscle weakness

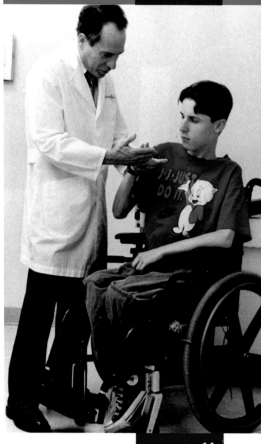

A boy with muscular dystrophy is examined by his doctor.

can spread to involuntary muscles. The disease can affect the heart and lungs. But that doesn't happen with everyone who gets the disease.

Muscular dystrophy is a rare condition. Doctors estimate that 250,000 people in the United States have MD. **Duchenne muscular dystrophy**, the most common type in children, affects 1 in 3,000 boys and almost no girls. And 1 in 3,000 people, both male and female, has **myotonic MD**, another form of the disease.

Types of MD

Doctors have identified at least nine types of muscular dystrophy. The major forms of MD differ from one another. Some forms start in childhood, some during young adulthood, and others in old age. Some break down muscles quickly, while others take a long time. Different forms of MD affect different parts of the body.

All forms of MD have one thing in common: They are all **genetic diseases**. That means they're passed on within families, from parents to children.

Myotonic Muscular Dystrophy

Myotonic MD is the most common form of muscular dystrophy in adults of both sexes. This is the type the Parkers have.

Myotonic MD is most often an adult disease, but not always. It usually starts between the ages of 20 and 40. It can cause a slow weakening of muscles in the face, hands, feet, legs, and neck. Affected muscles become stiff, especially after they're used.

People can live for many years with this disease. As with other forms of MD, people with myotonic MD feel weak. Their legs and arms are likely to be thin, because their muscles get smaller and weaker as the disease progresses.

Louise Parker has these symptoms: Her legs, arms, back, and lungs all are weak. She loses her balance easily and trips over small things, and then she has a hard time getting up. Swallowing and chewing are sometimes difficult for her. And, at times, her heart races.

The leg braces Scott Parker wears prevent him from walking on tiptoe and falling down. He has some problems keeping his balance. Like his mother, he is thin.

The Parkers' symptoms have taken 20 years to develop. For the first several years after being diagnosed with the disease, Scott and his mother could walk without braces or support.

Myotonic MD is passed on by certain **genes**—the coded material we inherit from our parents. Anyone who inherits the gene will have the disease. About half the children of a parent with the gene for myotonic MD can be expected to inherit that gene.

Doctors have recently discovered something interesting about myotonic MD. Unlike most other genetic diseases, it can get worse from one generation to the next. The gene that causes it can change between parent and child.

Duchenne Muscular Dystrophy

Duchenne muscular dystrophy is the most common form of MD that affects children. It was named for a French doctor, Guillaume Duchenne, who wrote about the disease in 1868.

Children with Duchenne MD usually learn to walk normally. Then, between ages 3 and 5, they start having problems. Their leg muscles and pelvises become weak. Their weak legs often cause what doctors call a "waddling gait," which makes them sway from side to side when they walk. When they get older, Duchenne children often have curved backs, a condition called **scoliosis**. Their legs often look chubby because fat fills in where muscle is supposed to be.

Almost everyone who has Duchenne muscular dystrophy is a boy. That's because the gene that causes it goes from mothers to sons.

Duchenne MD gets worse more quickly than many other kinds of MD. By the time they are 12 or 13, most boys with Duchenne are in wheelchairs. Their muscles keep getting weaker. Later, their breathing and their lungs—which are controlled by involuntary muscles—are affected. Because of these problems, most people with Duchenne MD die before they turn 30.

That's one reason researchers are looking so hard to find a cure for this form of muscular dystrophy. People who raise money to fight MD, like Jerry Lewis, spend a lot of time talking about Duchenne MD. This is the disease most people think of when they hear the words *muscular dystrophy*.

Michael's Story

Michael Norton's parents say he had trouble learning to walk, but they expected that. Because of a birth defect that was unrelated to MD, his feet had to be operated on when he was young. When he did learn to walk, he had stiff legs and fell down a lot.

Because Michael was frequently sick, he was tested by several doctors. When he was 4 years old, his parents were told that he had Duchenne MD. A test had shown that a certain kind of muscle protein was missing from Michael's blood—a sure sign of this form of MD.

Michael is 6 now, and he can still walk. But he has a hard time walking up and down stairs. His parents massage and stretch his leg muscles twice a week to help strengthen them.

Michael is smart and goes to regular first grade. He likes to play with his younger brother, John. He can ride a bike with training wheels and is learning to swim. He can still walk without leg braces. But his muscles are getting weaker all the time.

Michael has to be careful during flu season. Like many people with a serious disease, a cold or the flu can be danger-ous for him. He gets flu shots every year.

Michael Norton, who has muscular dystrophy, has his legs massaged by his mother, Susan, to keep them loose during therapy.

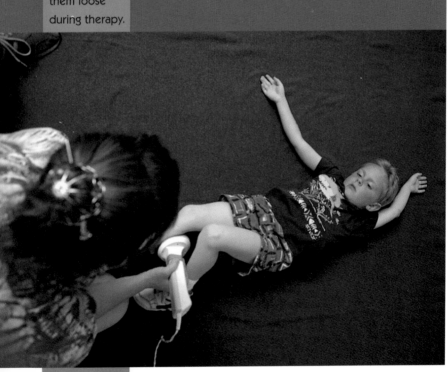

Becker Muscular Dystrophy

Becker MD is like Duchenne, except it is less severe and often begins later in life. Some people are already in their twenties when they get Becker MD. It affects the same parts of the body as Duchenne and in the same ways. But it takes much longer to get worse. Boys and young men with Becker muscular dystrophy can live longer than those with Duchenne.

Limb-Girdle Muscular Dystrophy

Limb-girdle MD affects mainly the muscles of the pelvic area at the top of the legs (the pelvic girdle). Both children and adults can get the disease, but it is usually worse when it starts at an early age.

Symptoms are similar to those of Duchenne and Becker MD, but people with limb-girdle MD usually live longer. This form of MD is passed on to both boys and girls. People can carry the gene without having the disease.

Less Common Forms of MD

There are five other forms of muscular dystrophy. The most common of the five types is listed first; the least common is listed last.

Facioscapulohumeral: Facioscapulohumeral MD usually affects the face and shoulders first. Patients may have trouble raising their arms over their heads or doing simple things like closing their eyes tightly or puffing their cheeks. Over time, the disease usually weakens the muscles in the torso and legs. Twenty percent of those affected end up in a wheelchair. This form of MD affects boys and girls. It most often starts in the teen years or young adulthood and gets worse slowly.

Congenital: This form of MD begins at birth and gets worse slowly, if at all. It can affect all parts of the body and can affect boys and girls. It weakens the muscles, and in the worst cases, the muscles become deformed. In other cases, though, the disease is very mild and does not worsen at all.

Oculopharyngeal: Often the first symptom of this form of MD is drooping eyelids, caused by a weakening of muscles in the face. This kind of MD usually begins in older men and women, ages 40 to 70, and gets worse slowly.

Distal: This form of MD also affects adults. It usually affects the hands first, making it hard to pick up things. People's feet and legs may get weak later. The disease usually spreads slowly.

Emery-Dreifuss: This form of MD causes shortening of the muscles of the elbows, knees, shoulders, and ankles and, sometimes, an abnormal heartbeat. It only affects boys.

So far, there is no cure for any form of muscular dystrophy.

Who Gets Muscular Dystrophy?

Muscular dystrophy is not like a cold, the flu, or chickenpox. You can't catch it from being near someone who has the disease.

MD is a genetic disease. The only people who get it are those whose families pass on to them the gene or genes that cause it.

Genes are the coded material that controls what we will be like. They determine the color of our eyes and hair. They direct whether we'll look more like our father or our mother. Sometimes they determine what kinds of diseases we will have. They are like the program in a computer.

Genetic diseases are almost always passed on in one of three ways: by **dominant genes**, by **recessive genes**, or by **X-linked genes**.

This graphic shows how genetically linked traits, including diseases such as Muscular Dystrophy, are passed from generation to generation.

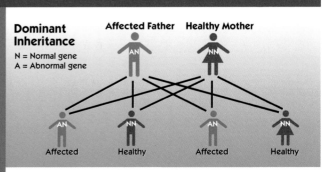

Dominant Inheritance

N = Normal gene
A = Abnormal gene

Affected Father
AN

Healthy Mother
NN

AN
Affected

NN
Healthy

AN
Affected

NN
Healthy

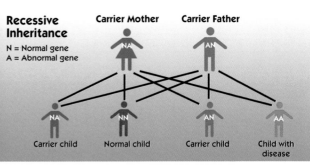

Recessive Inheritance

N = Normal gene
A = Abnormal gene

Carrier Mother
NA

Carrier Father
AN

NA
Carrier child

NN
Normal child

AN
Carrier child

AA
Child with disease

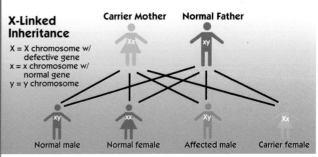

X-Linked Inheritance

X = X chromosome w/ defective gene
x = x chromosome w/ normal gene
y = y chromosome

Carrier Mother
Xx

Normal Father
xy

xy
Normal male

xx
Normal female

Xy
Affected male

Xx
Carrier female

Dominant Genes

For each gene you inherit from your mother, you inherit a matching gene from your father. Those two genes—or sometimes a combination of genes—determine your traits. For example, if you get a gene for brown eyes from your mother and a gene for blue eyes from your father, you will probably have brown eyes. That is because the gene for brown eyes—the dominant gene—is stronger than the gene for blue eyes—the recessive gene.

Diseases that are passed on through dominant genes, such as myotonic muscular dystrophy, usually show up in every generation of a family. That's because every person who inherits the defective gene from a parent will have the disease. It "dominates" over the matching, but normal, gene from the other parent.

Recessive Genes

Diseases passed on by recessive genes can catch families by surprise. That's because a recessive gene can "hide" in people who inherit the gene. If they also inherit a matching gene that is normal, that normal gene dominates. So they don't get the disease. But they can pass it on to their children.

A child must inherit two recessive genes to have the disease. It works the same way for eye color and certain other traits. If you have blue eyes, chances are you got the genes for blue eyes from both your father and your mother. But both your parents could have brown eyes. They could each carry one gene for brown eyes and one gene for blue eyes.

Conditions passed on by recessive genes are usually less common than those handed down through dominant genes. The kinds of muscular dystrophy that are passed on through recessive genes include limb-girdle and congenital muscular dystrophy.

X-Linked Genes

Like hair color and other traits, a person's sex is determined by genetic information from one's parents. Each of us inherits two sex **chromosomes** (strings of genes): one from our mother and one from our father. Women have two X chromosomes, so every child they have—boy or girl—will inherit an X chromosome from the mother. Men, though, have an X chromosome and a Y chromosome. If a man passes along a Y chromosome, the child will be a boy.

Diseases like Duchenne MD almost always strike boys. The recessive gene that causes such diseases is on the X chromosome. In a girl who inherits the Duchenne gene, the faulty gene is dominated by the healthy gene on her other X chromosome.

But boys have no other X chromosome. So if a boy inherits the gene from his mother, he will have the disease.

A common example of an X-linked condition is color blindness. Girls rarely have color blindness, but they can inherit the gene and pass it on to their children. Boys who get the gene, however, will have trouble telling some colors apart.

Other forms of muscular dystrophy that are X-linked are Becker and Emery-Dreifuss.

Sometimes a genetic disease is passed on by a parent who does not carry the gene. Something happens while the baby is forming, and the gene mutates, or changes.

For example, when Michael Norton, whose story is told in Chapter 2, was diagnosed with Duchenne MD, his mother's blood was studied. Doctors found out she did not carry the Duchenne gene. They told her that Michael was the victim of a mutation. Like many other diseases, it just happened, and doctors don't know why yet. Researchers are learning new things about inherited diseases all the time.

Chapter 4

Living with Muscular Dystrophy

When your grandparents were children, a boy like Michael Norton, who became weak because of muscular dystrophy, didn't have much chance to have fun. He would most likely have been put in a wheelchair, and his parents and other people would have waited on him. They might have helped him with the simplest tasks, like eating. He would have lost his strength faster because he wouldn't have been allowed to do anything for himself.

Today, therapists, doctors, and parents do everything they can to help children and adults with MD enjoy their lives. That includes letting them do things for themselves.

If you lifted weights every day for a year, your arms would get stronger. In a way, the same thing is true of people with muscular dystrophy. The more they use their affected muscles, the stronger those muscles will remain.

That's one reason Michael and the Parkers still walk instead of using wheelchairs. The longer they can walk, the

Michael Norton prepares to hit the ball during a game of T-ball.

stronger they will be. When people with muscular dystrophy need help, though, they can turn to many kinds of specialists.

Physical Therapists

Physical therapists work with doctors to help patients stay in good physical shape. People with muscular dystrophy go to physical therapists for exercises that help the muscles and the spine. Most of the exercises involve some kind of stretching. Therapists sometimes help MD patients practice walking with their feet flat on the ground and their bodies straight.

Occupational Therapists

Simple tasks can be hard to perform if your muscles are getting weaker all the time. Patients with muscular dystrophy are often sent to **occupational therapists**—specialists trained to help with everyday activities.

At a school like Scott Parker's, occupational therapists encourage children with MD to dress themselves, brush their teeth, feed themselves, and do other tasks to take care of themselves. If an older person's hand muscles are weakened by MD, an occupational therapist might help that person practice turning door-knobs or buttoning buttons.

Speech and Swallowing Therapists

Speech therapy is often recommended for MD patients who have difficulty talking clearly. The muscles in the face and neck are sometimes affected by the disease. By having patients practice different sounds, speech therapists can help them improve their ability to talk.

Some problems caused by muscular dystrophy need special help. For example, patients who have trouble swallowing may be unable to eat, drink, and breathe properly. A swallowing therapist can help them change their habits by teaching them new ways to swallow.

Other Types of Help

Eventually, most people with the more serious kinds of muscular dystrophy have a hard time walking without some kind of help. When that happens, they use leg braces—hard plastic bands that strap onto the legs. The braces hold the legs steady when weakened muscles can't support the

Kelly Rose Mahoney, 1994 MDA National Goodwill Ambassador, prepares to ride a pony. Mahoney, who has spinal muscular dystrophy, wears braces on her lower legs to help her walk.

legs anymore. Braces are the closest thing to new muscles for an MD patient.

When leg braces are no longer enough, many people with MD use walkers. A walker is a metal frame that supports the body as the person takes steps. Later, patients may use motorized carts or wheelchairs. They can go many places in wheelchairs, but there are barriers. Stairs, heavy doors, or high curbs can be a stop sign for someone in a wheelchair.

Louise Parker says she plans to keep walking with braces for as long as possible because wheelchairs make life harder. Even with braces, she says, she sometimes faces obstacles. Some people let heavy doors slam in her face; other people have turned away when she's fallen and needed help getting on her feet.

But most people are helpful, and things are changing for the disabled. Schools and other public places—like town halls and many stores, buses, and houses of worship—are required by law to have ramps alongside stairs and doors wide enough for wheelchairs to enter.

Since 1992, businesses with at least 25 workers have been required to remodel their buildings so handicapped people, including those in wheelchairs, can enter. The **Americans with Disabilities Act (ADA)** also forbids employers from discriminating because of physical disabilities. If people are qualified for jobs, for example, they can't be turned down just because they can't walk.

When the ADA was signed into law, one U.S. senator called it "the twentieth-century Emancipation Proclamation." Like the act that freed the slaves, the ADA told people with disabilities that they have the right to lead normal lives.

Some disabled people say that this kind of progress is just as important as research to find cures for diseases like MD. If schools, stores, workplaces, and recreational areas are open to people in wheelchairs, then being in a wheelchair would be seen as a difference, not a disability.

Researchers are exploring new ways to help people with MD live on their own. A California group called Canine Companions for Independence trains dogs to do simple jobs for disabled people. Some children with MD are using the dogs.

A canine helper can fetch a lunch bag, turn on lights, carry books, open doors, and retrieve things from high shelves. Like seeing-eye dogs, the helper dogs are allowed in places where pets wouldn't be permitted. They are allowed to go to school with their owners.

David Klock, a Pennsylvania man in his thirties who is in a wheelchair as a result of muscular dystrophy, has a helper dog, Candy. He says she opens doors, answers the phone, carries items, and helps David exercise. She goes with him to his job as an engineer at a U.S. Navy plant.

Canine helper Morgan assists Larry Christie, a Morris County, New Jersey, Probation Officer, at his job.

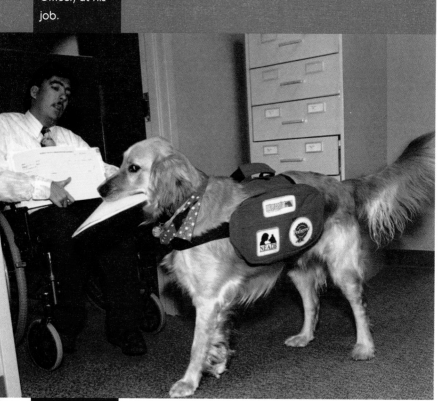

David was diagnosed with facioscapulo-humeral MD when he was 12. Now, more than 20 years later, he says, "I do more than a lot of able-bodied people I know." Candy, his dog companion, helps.

Respect for Those with MD

According to Louise Parker, thinking positively can be a big help for people with MD. Louise also appreciates people who take the time to understand her disease. Louise's worst days happen when people close doors in her face. It's hard for her, too, when people talk to her husband but not to her, as if she were incapable of understanding what was being said. She says sometimes people seem surprised when she tells them she graduated from high school.

The best times, she says, are when people treat her with the respect and dignity all humans deserve.

"There are lots of times when I get disgusted," she says. But then there are summer mornings when she has a chance to get out in the yard and plant flowers—by herself.

Chapter 5

Research into Muscular Dystrophy

Scientists are like detectives. For years they have been hunting for answers to questions about MD. What causes it? Why does one type of the disease attack muscles differently from another type? What can be done to treat or prevent the disease? They have made some discoveries and are hot on the trail of others.

In 1986, researchers found the genetic mutation responsible for Duchenne MD and Becker MD. A year later, they learned that the normal gene tells the body to make a protein called **dystrophin**. Healthy muscles all contain dystrophin, which helps them work.

Scientists learned that the mutated dystrophin gene doesn't do its job. In people with Duchenne, the body makes no dystrophin, and the muscles start to get weak while the person is still young. In Becker patients, the gene makes some dystrophin, but not enough.

Those discoveries led to tests that families with a history of either form of MD can take. Women can learn whether they carry the gene for Duchenne or Becker. Doctors can learn for sure whether a boy has Duchenne or Becker.

A woman who knows she carries the Duchenne or Becker gene can have her baby's blood tested before the baby is born. Then she will know whether her baby is going to get muscular dystrophy.

Other discoveries have led to a better understanding of how MD works. In 1992, scientists learned more about the way diseases are inherited. A parent with a genetic disease usually passes that disease to his or her children. But with myotonic muscular dystrophy, genes can change from one generation to the next. The children of a person with mild myotonic MD may inherit a stronger version of the same disease. The problem genes may increase from one generation to the next.

That's what happened with the family of Louise Parker. Neither of her parents seemed to have myotonic MD. Her father thought his aunt had it, because of the strange way she walked. But back then, no one in the family knew about the disease.

Doctors think Louise Parker's father had a mild form of MD. He passed it on to all four of his children. Each child had a worse case than the father. Louise's son, Scott, has a worse case than she has. While Louise did not get sick until she was in her thirties, Scott was sick at birth.

The first way a doctor decides whether someone has MD is by observing the person. The doctor watches the way the person walks, sits, and gets up from a chair. Usually a doctor tests the person's muscles to see why he or she is feeling weak or stiff.

If MD is suspected, the doctor will give the person a blood test. The test will tell whether the person has certain enzymes, or blood materials. One special kind of enzyme is found in high levels in the blood of boys with Duchenne and Becker muscular dystrophies.

A test called an electromyogram studies the way a person's muscles work. It prints a chart, like the pictures taken of heartbeats in electrocardiograms. Doctors can usually tell by looking at the chart whether a person has MD.

Another test that scientists have developed is called a **muscle biopsy**. In that test, a piece of muscle about the size of a fingertip is studied under a microscope. Healthy muscle looks quite different from muscle affected by MD. Sometimes muscle biopsies can show doctors which form of muscular dystrophy the person has.

Looking for a Treatment

Scientists are working hard to find a cure for muscular dystrophy. In 1990, researchers started testing a method they hoped would lead to a treatment. In the tests, healthy muscle cells that were still growing were injected into the muscles of a person with MD. Scientists hoped the healthy cells would keep growing, making the weak muscles stronger.

The tests continue, but the results have been disappointing. It is hard to put healthy cells in all the places where a person's muscles are weak. Everyone's body is different. When the cells from one person are put into another person, they can be rejected. The body of the person with muscular dystrophy can tell the difference between its own cells and someone else's. It wants to kick out the intruder cells.

Another kind of test began in 1993 at the University of Michigan. Scientists injected a gene for dystrophin, the healthy muscle protein, into mice with the Duchenne gene. The mice did not get MD. They stayed healthy.

This is exciting news. But doctors note that mice and people aren't the same. Many years of experiments with mice must be done before the method can be tested on people. Still, scientists are hopeful that someday a cure will be found.

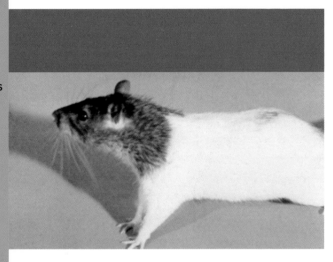

This mouse has been specially bred with the muscular dystrophy gene. Scientists use mice such as this to study the disease and search for cures.

Chapter 6

Helping People with MD

The **Muscular Dystrophy Association (MDA)** is the major organization raising funds to fight muscular dystrophy. It is one of the largest and best-organized charities in the United States.

The MDA pays for research with the millions of dollars it raises each year. It also provides services to people with MD and their families. And it educates the public about muscular dystrophy.

The MDA was formed in 1950 by a group of parents who were hoping to find treatments or cures for their children's disease. At that time, according to the

MDA, only one doctor in the United States had a practice devoted to fighting diseases like MD.

The MDA spent $20 million in 1993 on research into muscular dystrophy and 31 other muscle diseases. Scientists funded by MDA have made discoveries about diseases such as amyotrophic lateral sclerosis, often called Lou Gehrig's disease (a fatal disease that affects the spinal cord and causes muscular weakness), as well as MD.

More than 400 teams of scientists and doctors use money from the MDA to study muscle diseases. Their discoveries have sometimes led to better understanding of diseases that have nothing to do with MD—such as Alzheimer's disease (a brain disease that destroys the ability to think, feel, remember, and care for oneself) and cataracts. They have also made major discoveries about Duchenne, Becker, and myotonic muscular dystrophies.

In 1992, Edwin G. Krebs and Edmond H. Fisher, two scientists who had worked for years with the MDA, won the Nobel Prize in medicine. They were honored for their discovery of the way cells malfunction in diseases like MD. The Nobel Prize is one of the highest honors awarded to researchers.

The MDA runs about 240 clinics around the country. People with MD and their families receive a number of services at the clinics. Individuals can be diagnosed there.

Later they can get checkups, flu shots, and therapy at the clinics. Also, women who think they carry the gene for Duchenne or Becker MD can get tested. The clinics have wheelchairs, leg braces, and walkers for MD patients. The equipment is often free for patients who can't afford it.

Living with a **progressive disease** like MD—a disease that keeps getting worse—can be very hard on a family. Mothers, fathers, sisters, and brothers of patients can get counseling through MDA clinics. They are encouraged to talk about how they feel. For instance, the brother or sister of an MD patient may feel angry that the sick family member gets so much of their parents' attention.

The MDA runs 77 summer camps for children with MD. There, young people can learn new skills, spend time outside, and get a break from their daily routines.

The MDA also publishes booklets that explain what muscular dystrophy is and what can be done to help patients. There are books for brothers and sisters about how it

A boy plays ball at a summer camp for children with muscular dystrophy.

feels to have a sick family member.

In 1966 the MDA began holding telethons. Singers, dancers, and other entertainers perform, and people with MD talk about the disease while viewers are asked to call in with pledges of money. As of 1993, the telethons had raised more than $650 million.

Jerry Lewis is the MDA's national chairman. He has hosted the Labor Day telethons since they began. His name is so linked with MD that people with the disease are often called "Jerry's kids."

In the early 1990s, activists for the disabled complained about Lewis. They said he makes telethon viewers feel sorry for

Muscular Dystrophy Association's 1995 National Goodwill Ambassador, Thomas Diaz, with actor/comedian Jerry Lewis, who is the national chairman of MDA

people with MD instead of helping them understand what life with MD is like. Some activists noted that most people with MD are not children but adults who can live full and useful lives.

Some of the critics who have MD said they don't need to be cured. What they need, they said, is better access to places where able-bodied people can go. And they need respect from everyone. Cris Matthews, a former MDA poster child, said she objects to "the attitude that stresses that no matter what one does, life is meaningless in a wheelchair."

According to the MDA, Jerry Lewis has done more than anybody else to help people with muscular dystrophy. But the organization has paid attention to some of the critics. It has included more profiles of adults in its telethons. In 1992, it formed a committee of successful adults who have MD or other muscle diseases. Members of the National Task Force on Public Awareness who have muscular dystrophy include a number of successful professionals: a real estate consultant, a neurologist (a doctor who treats nerve diseases), the owner of a graphic arts firm, a college administrator, a woman who travels around the country talking about disabilities, and an electronics engineer with the U.S. Navy. Even Lewis's critics have agreed that the MDA does more than any other group to unlock the secrets of muscular dystrophy.

Another group that has helped people with MD is the Shriners Hospitals for Crippled Children. The Shriners run a network of 19 hospitals around the country. The hospitals provide free help to children with physical disabilities, including muscular dystrophy. They offer physical and occupational therapy and perform surgery on children whose backs have become curved by muscular dystrophy.

Support groups can help people who are living with MD. The Facio-Scapulo-Humeral Society in Massachusetts assists people who have that rare disease. It also provides information about FSH and hopes to push for more research. Canine Companions for Independence and other groups train dogs to serve disabled people. As mentioned in Chapter 4, these dogs can help people with muscular dystrophy live more independently. Canine Partners for Life, a small group in Pennsylvania, has a long waiting list for helper dogs. Families and friends can be the biggest help to people with muscular dystrophy. Children learn to do more for themselves if they are

A boy with muscular dystrophy plays with a camp counselor at a summer camp for children with MD.

encouraged by others. Doing more makes them feel better about themselves. That is why programs like canine helpers and adaptive sports (games for children with disabilities) are so important.

The Muscular Dystrophy Association urges people to remember some things about those with MD:

- They didn't do anything wrong to get the disease; it just happened.
- Most can do anything other people can do with their heads and hands.
- Most are not retarded.
- Many people can live for decades with MD.
- People with MD, just like anyone else, need love, encouragement, and understanding.

Louise Parker says she hopes her son, who has MD, will continue to walk and do things for himself for as long as he can. She hopes the same for herself as she lives with the disease.

It's important not to accept limitations and give up, she says. "You have to fight it every step of the way."

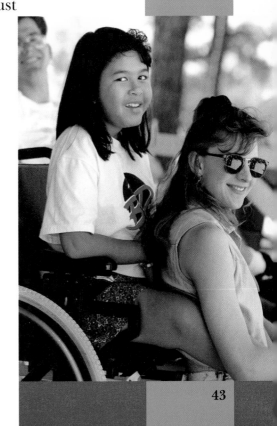

A young girl with muscular dystrophy enjoys a laugh with a camp counselor.

For Further Reading

Azarnoff, Pat. *Health, Illness and Disability: A Guide for Children and Young Adults.* New York: R. R. Bowker, 1983.

Franks, Hugh. *Will to Live.* New York: Routledge, 1979.

Kremetz, Jill. *How It Feels to Live with a Disability.* New York: Simon & Schuster, 1992.

Meyer, Donald, Rebecca Fewell, and Patricia Vadasky. *Living with a Brother or Sister with Special Needs.* Seattle: University of Washington Press, 1985.

Morrison, Velma. *There's Only One You: The Story of Heredity.* New York: Messner, 1978.

Osofsky, Audrey. *My Buddy.* New York: Henry Holt, 1992.

Roy, Ron. *Move Over, Wheelchairs Coming Through.* New York: Clarion Books, 1985.

Sirof, Harriet. *The Road Back: Living with a Physical Disability.* New York: New Discovery Books, 1993.

For More Information

Canine Companions for Independence
P.O. Box 466
Santa Rosa, CA 95402
(707) 528–0830
This organization trains dogs to be helpers
for disabled people, including those with
MD.

FSH Society
3 Westwood Road
Lexington, MA 02173
(617) 860–0501
Offers information about facioscapulohumeral MD and support for those who
have it.

Muscular Dystrophy Association
3300 East Sunset Drive
Tucson, AZ 85718–3208
(800) 572–1717
The major fund-raising and information
organization for MD. Regional offices are in
most states and are listed in the phone
book.

Shriners Hospitals for Crippled Children
2900 Rocky Point Drive
Tampa, FL 33607–1435
(800) 237–5055 (or 800–282–9161 in
Florida)
Hospitals that provide free services to children with disabilities, including MD

Glossary

Americans With Disabilities Act (ADA) A 1992 federal law that guarantees people with disabilities the right to access and jobs.

Becker muscular dystrophy A form of muscular dystrophy similar to Duchenne except that Becker MD often starts later in life and takes longer to worsen. It affects boys.

chromosome A string of genes.

congenital muscular dystrophy A type of MD that begins at birth. (The word *congenital* means "starting at birth.")

distal muscular dystrophy A mild form of MD that usually starts in adulthood.

dominant gene The stronger gene that usually controls or determines an inherited trait.

Duchenne muscular dystrophy The most common childhood form of MD. It affects boys and usually leads to death before age 30.

dystrophin A protein found in healthy muscles.

Emery-Dreifuss muscular dystrophy A rare form of MD that affects boys. It usually weakens muscles in the upper body first.

facioscapulohumeral muscular dystrophy A slowly progressing form of MD that often affects face muscles and usually comes on in teen or young adult years.

genes The coded material that determines how we will look and, sometimes, what illnesses we'll get.

genetic diseases Illnesses that are passed on through families and are not contagious.

involuntary muscles Muscles that work automatically and are not controlled by choice.

leg braces Plastic supports that are worn on the legs of people with MD and some other diseases. They help support weak muscles.

leg-girdle muscular dystrophy A form of MD that causes weakness mainly in the shoulder and hip areas and affects both males and females.

muscle biopsy A test that examines a piece of muscle to determine if a person has MD.

muscular dystrophy (MD) A genetic disease that causes slow weakening of the muscles.

Muscular Dystrophy Association (MDA) The major fund-raising, educational, and research organization for muscular dystrophy.

myotonic muscular dystrophy The most common adult form of MD, marked by muscle stiffness.

occupational therapy Treatment that helps people with everyday tasks such as getting dressed.

oculopharyngeal muscular dystrophy A form of MD that strikes older people and usually affects face muscles.

physical therapy Treatment that helps people maintain muscle strength and flexibility.

progressive disease A disease that gets worse over time.

recessive gene The less powerful gene that usually stays hidden in the person who inherits it.

scoliosis Curving of the backbone that can affect boys with MD.

voluntary muscles Muscles that are controlled by choice. In muscular dystrophy, these muscles become weak and break down.

Index